WHY WE'RE ATTRACTED

Spiritual, Psycho[logical, and Physical]
Elements That [Draw Us] to Others

Shepherd Hoodwin

Summerjoy Press
Laguna Niguel, California

WHY WE'RE ATTRACTED
Spiritual, Psychological and Physical Elements That Draw Us to Others

Summerjoy Press
99 Pearl
Laguna Niguel CA 92677-4818

shoodwin@gmail.com
https://shepherdhoodwin.com

Copyright © 2016 by Shepherd Hoodwin

All rights reserved. No part of this publication may be reproduced, stored in a retrieval system, or transmitted, in any form or by any means, electronic, mechanical, photocopying, recording, or otherwise, without the prior written permission of the publisher, except by a reviewer, who may quote brief passages in a review.

ISBN: 9798605992530

Photograph of Shepherd Hoodwin by John Kilis.

CONTENTS

INTRODUCTION	1
MULTI-CAUSALITY	1
ENERGETIC BONDS	2
BIOLOGICAL DEFAULTS AND CULTURAL NORMS	3
THE MICHAEL TEACHINGS	7
I SPIRITUAL FACTORS IN ATTRACTION	9
1 ♡ AGREEMENTS AND LIFE PATH	10
2 ♡ SOUL CHEMISTRY	16
3 ♡ SOUL-LEVEL RELATIONSHIPS	17
4 ♡ MALE/FEMALE ENERGY RATIO	20
5 ♡ ROLES	22
6 ♡ SOUL AGES	26
7 ♡ OVERLEAVES	28
8 ♡ KARMA	32
9 ♡ ASTROLOGY	33
10 ♡ VIBRATIONAL RESONANCE	35
11 ♡ CELIBACY AND UNION	38

II PSYCHOLOGICAL FACTORS IN ATTRACTION — 47

12 ♡ FINDING BALANCE — 48

13 ♡ PARENTS — 52
- TAKING RESPONSIBLILITY — 52
- WE CHOSE OUR PARENTS — 53
- FATHER AND MOTHER GOD — 54
- PICTURES OF REALITY — 56
- INCOMPLETION — 58
- TEMPLATES — 59

14 ♡ RESOLVING THE PAST — 62

III PHYSICAL FACTORS IN ATTRACTION — 67

15 ♡ BODY-TYPE ATTRACTION — 68

16 ♡ YOUR "TYPE" — 84

17 ♡ SEXUAL ORIENTATION — 88
- BISEXUALITY — 94

18 ♡ MONOGAMY AND POLYFIDELITY — 99

CONCLUSION — 102

ABOUT THE AUTHOR — 104

OTHER BOOKS BY SHEPHERD HOODWIN — 106

REVIEWS — 111

INTRODUCTION

Being in love is one of the great highs of life, yet it is often elusive or ephemeral. Unrequited love is a common theme of songs, and almost everyone experiences it on both sides. Just why are we attracted to some people and not to others?

There are many possible reasons for attraction and many different kinds of attraction, both within the sphere of romance and outside of it. On the surface, they can all seem like the same thing—we just know that we feel attracted. But attraction can be primarily physical, emotional, mental, or spiritual. Our inner child may be attracted to someone's playfulness, while our body isn't particularly attracted to his, and our inner parent may cringe at his lack of responsibility—attraction often isn't consistent. We might have a friendship dynamic with someone but try to make it into a romantic one.

MULTI-CAUSALITY

The concept of multi-causality is that often several factors converge to create a situation. There can be many causes for being attracted to someone, just as there can be many for a life issue, illness, or event. Forces can be at work on multiple levels. When we settle for just one explanation of anything complex, we miss much of the picture.

Being able to identify the elements of our attraction to someone can help us be clearer on what the relationship has and doesn't have. No relationship will cover all the bases, but if we're also clear on what is essential for us in a long-term relationship and what is negotiable, we will be better able to decide. Ultimately, it will probably come down to a gut feeling—the overall gestalt of the relationship either works for us or it doesn't. Having an intellectual framework, however, can help us avoid talking ourselves into something because we're tired of waiting or because our buttons—emotional, mental, or physical—are pushed. Biology doing its hormonal job can cast a spell that leads to choices we later regret. The spell is magical and worth enjoying while it lasts but alone isn't enough on which to base important decisions. People who quickly fall in and out of love aren't really dealing with love in any spiritual sense but with shifts in body chemistry, most likely.

ENERGETIC BONDS

Ideally, a romantic relationship contains many levels of attraction. If we're attuned to energy fields, we can observe where, in general, the attractions are between a couple by looking at their energetic lines of connection. For example, if they share a soul connection, they will likely connect at their hearts and crowns. If they connect at their heads and not too much at their gonads or anywhere else, their relationship is probably primarily intellectual—they might have great, enriching conversations—even if it's also a sexual relationship. If they mostly connect at their gonads, it's likely to be primarily a sexual relationship, without much intellectual, emotional, or spiritual sharing.

Frequently, connections are not straight across. For example, one person's gonads may connect energetically with the other's head. In that case, the first person might be turned on sexually by the other person's mind.

In a mature, well-balanced relationship, there's a full, strong energy exchange. The more true this is, the more the couple will feel oneness. It's unlikely that any couple connects fully on all levels, but as a relationship grows and deepens, the connections increase in both quantity and quality.

There are many good resources available for helping develop intuitive or psychic perception of energy, such as books by John Friedlander including *Psychic Psychology: Energy Skills for Life and Relationships*.

BIOLOGICAL DEFAULTS AND CULTURAL NORMS

There are several "default settings" when it comes to physical attraction that govern unless a person has reason to override them. For example, bodies usually feel more comfortable sexually with other bodies that are in the same age range. For one thing, that better suits biology's reproductive goals. (A woman of child-bearing age needs a mate who will likely be around to help raise her children.) For another, there is an inherent comfort with what is similar—it's familiar—although there can be fascination or excitement with what is different.

However, there are good reasons why people occasionally override this default. It is usually assumed that someone who prefers much older partners is looking for a mother or father substitute, and someone who prefers much younger partners is seeking his youth or is stuck at a younger age. This is not necessarily the case. Sometimes factors such as age or even gender seem to disappear when two people are drawn to each other for other reasons.

In exploring the spiritual side of relationships, the premise of this book is that each of us is an eternal soul who plans each lifetime before incarnating, including making agreements with other souls. [For more information, please see my book *Journey of Your Soul: A Channel Explores the Michael Teachings*.] There are a number of spiritual factors that could attract someone to a different age range. Perhaps two souls who happen to be of different ages have agreements that can best be fulfilled sexually. A person whose life task is to mentor may be attracted to younger partners; a person whose life task is to bridge generations, to older. Souls don't care much about biological defaults and cultural norms—they have their own agendas.

If two people have a close soul bond such as that of essence twins (twin souls) or essence mates (both discussed in chapter 3), an age difference might not faze them. Mary Kay Letourneau is a former schoolteacher who began an affair with a student, Vili Fualaau, when he was twelve-years-old and she was thirty-four. She went to prison for it and married him when she got out. Their determination to be together no matter the cost reflects the fact that they are essence mates and have a mate agreement, according to my channeling of Michael (discussed in the next section).

Often, biological defaults become enshrined as cultural norms. To some degree, our culture tolerates relationships between older men and younger women—that seems to underline men's dominance, virility, and perhaps wealth—but is less accepting of the reverse.

Many people are offended by relationships that violate cultural norms without really being able to say why. One reason is that we are biologically hardwired to ensure survival by creating clans. We hold them together by enforcing conformity (with gossip, for instance). As consciousness evolves, we can transcend these primitive mechanisms with reason and love, and can therefore be more flexible. Studies have shown that conservative people are more governed by fear, and fear causes people to revert to the seeming safety of defaults and norms. Progressives tend to believe that people should be free to do what they wish as long as they don't cause real harm.

Cultural norms are created partly by familiarity, since we tend to fear the unknown, but they change over time. Throughout history, there has been pressure on young people to marry those of similar socioeconomic, religious, and ethnic backgrounds. Miscegenation (mating between people of different races) was still criminalized in sixteen states before the Supreme Court struck down such laws in 1967. It wasn't that long ago that it was considered scandalous for a straight couple to live together without being married. Gay marriage has become accepted amazingly quickly. It probably won't be long before other forms of relationship such as polyfidelity (discussed in the final chapter) become accepted as well.

There is nothing sacred about biological defaults and cultural norms; fundamentally, they are just habits. Computers come from the factory with many default settings but it is our prerogative to change them.

Even with animals, there are exceptions to biological defaults. Heterosexuality is nature's default since it ensures survival through reproduction. A large majority of humans and animals are heterosexual. Still, the Wikipedia article "Homosexual behavior in animals" quotes scientist Petter Bøckman as saying, "No species has been found in which homosexual behaviour has *not* been shown to exist." This ruins the argument of the religious right that it isn't natural. The universe is an exuberant place that loves diversity and experimentation. The purpose of sex is more than just reproduction —it is about joy and union. Just because some behavior isn't in the majority, it doesn't mean it's not natural and healthy.

THE MICHAEL TEACHINGS

Many of the concepts here are from the channeled Michael teachings. Michael is a group of souls working cooperatively who have completed their lifetimes on the physical plane. If you're new to the teachings, my site (https://shepherdhoodwin.com) has a glossary, bibliography, and other information, although I have also included definitions in the text. You can order channeled

Michael Reading charts on yourself and loved ones here. They include your role, body type, and about twenty other items. Having that information can enrich your understanding of this material.

This book focuses on sexual/romantic attraction but most of what is covered applies to all kinds of relationships.

We're going to explore factors of attraction in three categories: spiritual (soul), psychological (personality), and physical (body).

PART I
SPIRITUAL FACTORS IN ATTRACTION

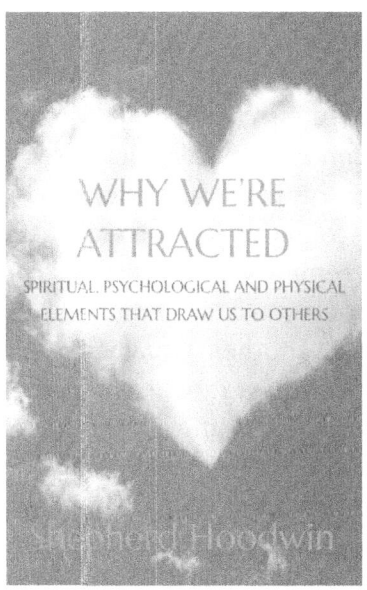

1 ♡ AGREEMENTS AND LIFE PATH

When we meet someone with whom we have a soul-level *agreement* (contract to do something together on the physical plane), we may have a surge of recognition and be attracted to that person. Agreements can be short or long term. In fact, an agreement could simply be to introduce one person to another. Usually agreements have nothing to do with sex, but if the person comes in the right "package" and we're in the market for a romantic relationship, it's easy to assume that the attraction is romantic. This can be a mistake. Just because we have an agreement or another soul connection, or we simply like someone a lot or get along well with him, it doesn't necessarily mean that we have the makings of romance.

1 AGREEMENTS AND LIFE PATH

First of all, there needs to be adequate physical attraction, but people who have been waiting a long time for the right person are sometimes willing to compromise on that, which usually doesn't work out in the long run. A few women have told me that physical attraction that was lacking for them grew as they bonded or fell in love, but I've never heard a man say that. Most people I've discussed this with, both male and female, say that if it's not there in the beginning, it's not going to be. For some people, however, physical attraction is a lesser priority and/or more flexible than for most, which was probably true for those women. The neutral solar body type, for example, is attracted to all body types (discussed in chapter 15). In any case, physical attraction is obviously important in romantic relationships, and it may not be a good idea to enter into one hoping that it will follow.

Even if there is physical attraction, our *life paths* also need to be able to fit together for a successful long-term relationship. We each make a *life plan* before incarnating, which includes our *life task* and agreements with other souls for accomplishing it. Our life path is the course our life takes as our plan unfolds. If our agreements call for us to live in a particular place because many souls with whom we have agreements are there, and the other person's call for him to be in a different place, it's not going to work. (Life plans don't necessarily require living in particular places but sometimes they do.) Someone with a high wanderlust because her agreements are in many places will probably not fit with a homebody. If our plan includes having several children and the other person's plan calls for being childless, that's probably a deal-breaker no matter how much love there is. Love alone is not enough. Eventually we'll all love each other, albeit in different ways—it has to work, too.

Among the many kinds of soul agreements we make, both before incarnating and during a lifetime, the one that directly concerns intimate relationships is the *mate agreement*. We normally make several (about nine is average) because we never know for sure before incarnating how things are going to work out—who will be where, doing what. By the time we're ready to mate, many may have already mated with someone else. Sometimes we meet someone available with whom we have a mate agreement but cross him or her off our list because, even though it works on the soul level, it doesn't on the personality level. Perhaps he became an alcoholic or she became a rigid fundamentalist. So we say, "Next!" and see if we can meet someone else on our list. Of course, we have shortcomings, too, so those with whom we have mate agreements may also cross us off their list.

Validating that a relationship works on the personality level is essential. Because the feminine

1 AGREEMENTS AND LIFE PATH

concerns the inner world, many women, especially, tend to fall in love with a person's soul and make too little of personality-level failings. However, it's the personality that we live with day-to-day. Often they hope he will change since they can clearly see his potential. It's best to assume WYSIWYG: What you see is what you get. People generally don't change dramatically in one lifetime, discounting things like becoming sober or doing intensive psychospiritual work. For example, if someone is a slob, he's not likely to become neat, so if that's important to us, it's wise to take it seriously and consider whether we can live with that never changing.

If no one else is currently available from our list of mate agreements, we go on to our backup list or see who else is out there. Agreements offer a framework but they aren't carved in stone. We as souls are flexible and are mainly concerned with accomplishing our life tasks in whatever ways work, sometimes reverting to Plan B, C, or D or just winging it. Having a mate agreement is not a requirement for having a fulfilling relationship and is not a guarantee of it either. For example, a mate agreement may be made in order to repay a karmic debt or to complete other agreements. Mate agreements aren't necessarily made because we fit hand and glove. Even if we do fit hand and glove on a soul level, that's no assurance that we will on a personality level. However, if we do have a mate agreement, we know that an intimate relationship works from the soul's point of view. It's like having a mortgage pre-approved—we won't necessarily buy the house, but if we decide to, the mortgage is in place.

I worked with someone who'd been through a large portion of her twenty mate agreements, crossing them off her list not necessarily because of their inadequacies but because of her own unavailability due to her fear of being vulnerable. She rationalized that it was their fault but she unconsciously sabotaged each potential relationship. Being a good mate is more important than finding one because whomever we're with, we're there, too, and we co-create our relationships.

A mate relationship can be a useful framework for completing agreements that, in themselves, have nothing to do with being mated. Agreements involving service to others may be especially suitable to mate relationships. Many couples are fulfilling agreements but have no mate agreement. That doesn't make their relationship less good or satisfying but it does probably suggest that it is not about mating per se; the mating is more a means to other ends such as accomplishing a particular task or lesson.

Our life is a combination of our soul's loosely framed plan and the free will of all concerned. The physical plane "school" is, in large part, about learning to make wise choices in light of how things

1 AGREEMENTS AND LIFE PATH

are, even when they don't seem to be going according to plan and we don't know what the future will bring (which we never really do anyway). It's disappointing when a relationship we had high hopes for doesn't work out, but all of our experiences can teach us and make us better equipped for those that follow. The important thing is to move on, firmly grounded in our intuition about what is right for us now, and now, and now....

[For more information about life plans, see my books *Journey of Your Soul* and *Being in the World*.]

2 ♡ SOUL CHEMISTRY

We make agreements with other souls because of our history together in past lives and between lives. Each pair of souls develops a pattern of relating. For example, one soul may continually stimulate us and/or push our buttons, whereas another may be comforting. One soul may frequently mate with us while another is often a sibling. One soul may often be our teacher and/or student and another, our friend. There are lifetimes that are exceptions to the rule, and soul relationships evolve and change—sometimes friendly souls decide to try mating, for instance. And some are versatile from the beginning. However, knowing our soul-level chemistry with another person can add an important piece to the puzzle. Ways to access this and other arcana include meditation, regression, and working with a channel or psychic. [Please see my site for information about readings.]

3 ♡ SOUL-LEVEL RELATIONSHIPS

Being in the same *cadence* (group of seven souls), *entity* (soul family of about a thousand or more souls), *cadre* (seven entities), or *cadre group* (twelve cadres, aka *energy ring*) can be responsible for providing an instant sense of recognition and connection upon meeting someone. Within cadres, those in neighboring entities feel especially allied, and those two apart (for example, entities two and four) are particularly complementary. It's similar among the cadres of a cadre group.

Ultimately, we're all one, but some connections are more direct than others. The majority of our agreements are with members of our cadre, and most of the rest are with members of other cadres of our cadre group. However, the unpredictable aspect of life means that occasionally we will meet and deeply bond with souls not in our cadre group, forming a *heart link*. Any significant past-life history with someone, regardless of soul group connections, can bring a strong sense of already knowing him upon meeting.

Our most powerful soul relationship is with our *essence twin*, a.k.a. *twin soul* or *twin flame*. (*Soul mate* is a broader term that can refer to this, or another soul with whom we have a mate agreement or an otherwise important and comfortable bond.) The second most powerful is our *task companion*. We may also have former essence twins (known as *essence mates*) and task companions (*task mates*) from previous *grand cycles* in different life forms on other planets; they feel similar but less intense than the current ones; we're often very close to them. These souls may or may not be incarnate when we are, and if they are, they may or may not be mate material. If we meet them at all, they could also be family members, friends, co-workers, "ships passing in the night," or even nemeses.

People tend to romanticize these connections, especially essence twins, but even if they're in the right "package" and we have mate agreements with them, there's, again, no guarantee that the relationship will work well. On the other hand, no relationship is more compelling or powerful than an essence twin romantic relationship that does work well. Such relationships are rare; for one thing, essence twins can create their own insular world together and miss out on other experiences, so souls don't often set it up to be together in this way. We don't even meet our essence twin in more than 10-30% of our lives.

The popular idea that we each have one true soul mate, our "other half," is based on the essence twin. The fact is, however, that souls crave variety and want to have many different kinds of mates. It takes on average over a hundred lifetimes to complete the physical plane, and some souls have many hundreds or even more. No matter how

3 SOUL-LEVEL RELATIONSHIPS

close a relationship is, eventually it would reach the limits of its growth potential.

4 ♡ MALE/FEMALE ENERGY RATIO

Each soul has a fixed ratio of male to female energy. In the Michael teachings, male energy specifically refers to linear energy that moves out into the world to achieve a goal; female energy is the opposite: it is atmospheric, process-oriented, and moves inward. For example, someone with high male energy is more likely to be career-oriented and can be a workaholic. Someone with high female energy tends to like being at home and creating an environment. A soul who has the opposite of our ratio is magnetic for us. The more extreme our ratio, the more compelling is the opposite.

I used to wonder what brought my parents together—they seemed mismatched. Then I channeled their Michael Reading charts and found that my mother's ratio was 23/77 and my father's was 77/23. They also had some body-type attraction, but not a lot. (There are also couples in

4 MALE/FEMALE ENERGY RATIO

which the man has higher female energy and the women, higher male, as well as same-sex couples with opposite ratios.)

My ratio is 47/53. Being so close to the middle, anyone else in the middle range can work for me, but someone at exactly 53/47 or close to that has an extra pull for me.

Role (soul type, discussed next) has more to do with what we think of as masculinity or femininity than male/female energy. For example, even a higher-female-energy warrior or king will probably seem more masculine in our culture than a high-male-energy artisan or server. In a culture with a lot of warrior women and artisan men, the opposite may seem true. Imprinting, body type, and many other factors also play a part in the perception of masculinity or femininity. However, all other things being equal, a high-male-energy sage, for example, will likely seem more masculine than a high-female-energy sage.

5 ♡ ROLES

We each have one of seven *roles* (soul types, or ways of being): *server* and *priest* are inspirational, *artisan* and *sage* are expressive, *warrior* and *king* are active, and *scholar* is assimilative. These are not just archetypes—each role is designed and operates differently. For more on the roles, see my site and michaelteachings.com, especially here and here.

We often see certain combinations together as couples. Scholars (the number four role) and warriors (number three) may be the most common. Many science fiction authors (and fans) are male scholars. To create those complex, detailed universes, one would almost have to be a scholar to have enough knowledge in diverse fields to pull it off. Their heroines are frequently warriors, whereas in other media such as movies, heroines are usually softer roles (although that's changing somewhat). Those scholar authors seem to look up at those strong warrior women with puppy-dog eyes; for them, they're the epitome of womanhood. Often the cover illustrations of heroines look like earthy warriors, with cool, focused eyes, demonstrating how people may associate soul types with looks even if they don't consciously know about roles.

The other role combinations whose numbers add up to seven are also classic combinations: servers

5 ROLES

(one) and priests (six), and artisans (two) and sages (five). (Sage writers are likely to write artisan romantic interests, and vice versa.) These two combinations also share their axis (universal quality)—servers and priests are on the inspiration axis, and sages and artisans are on the expression axis. That is another factor of comfort and attraction. Kings and warriors also get along well by reason of both being on the action axis.

Another common combination is kings and servers (with the caveat that kings only account for about four percent of the population). Kings are already the number seven role, so the number one role is the closest another person can come to adding up to seven for them. Kings also like being served, and servers especially like to serve kings.

Scholars and priests are also commonly attracted and are frequently essence twins, although not as commonly as scholars and warriors. Scholars, being the neutral role, are naturally attracted to the two most intense roles; warriors are intense in an earthy way, and priests in a spiritual way. Priests and warriors like it that scholars can absorb their excess energy, and scholars like the stimulation. (A similar dynamic occurs on a physical level between opposite body types, discussed in chapter 15.)

Warriors, the lowest frequency role, can be fascinated by the two high-frequency roles, artisans and priests, and vice versa, so there can be a lot of "opposites attract" chemistry, but the dishes can fly in those relationships.

Artisans and kings are the most foreign combination. It's not that they conflict so much that they tend to have little ability to understand one another—it's like they're from different planets.

Souls of the same role tend to get along well, with the possible exception of artisans, who often seek more stabilizing partners. We also tend to be especially attracted to those who have the same role as that of our essence twin when it's different from our own. A scholar with a server essence twin, for instance, will tend to be drawn to servers even though that's not usually a compelling combination.

Servers, artisans, and scholars tend to be pretty low-key, and relationships with them can be rather quiet (which may be just what one is looking for), especially when both roles are low-key. Relationships with kings and warriors can be galvanizing. Relationships with sages tend to be fun and stimulating. Relationships with priests are often warm and inspiring. Of course, there are exceptions to everything written here, and essence twin bleedthrough or even *casting* (our resonances with certain roles based on our position within our soul families) can bring in elements of attraction lacking in the roles themselves. [I cover this in much greater depth on my site and in *Journey of Your Soul*.]

6 ♡ SOUL AGES

There are five soul ages we experience on the physical plane: *infant, baby, young, mature,* and *old*. They roughly parallel human stages of development: newborn, toddler, youngster, adolescent, and young adult. The movement from infant to young climaxes in a sense of mastery of the outer world. Then, the soul turns a corner and dives in to the inner world, not unlike what occurs when adolescence hits.

There can be successful relationships between any combination of soul ages, but those of the same age have the advantage of seeing life from the same vantage point. Mature and old souls also usually get along well because both are inwardly focused; in addition, mature souls' intensity and old souls' casualness can balance one another. Similarly, baby and young souls are both outwardly focused, and the baby soul's emphasis on family and often religion can provide a foundation for the young soul's career orientation. A young soul's industry can balance an old soul's laissez-faire attitude about things such as earning a living but their difference in perspective can be stressful. Baby souls share mature souls' interest in community, although at a simpler level and without a desire to process emotions. They can have stable relationships that work fairly well, but baby souls can find mature souls complicated, and mature souls can be disappointed in baby souls' lack of emotional depth.

7 ♡ OVERLEAVES

When planning an individual lifetime, we choose several personality attributes, *overleaves*, that overlay our soul. They include our *goal* (primary motivator), *mode* (dominant way of operating), *attitude* (how we tend to view life), and *center* (the part of self from which we react). Just as there are seven roles, there are seven of each of the overleaves.

In the Michael teachings, traits are said to have positive and negative *poles*. In the positive poles, the energies manifest in a clear, love-based way; in the negative, they are distorted in some way by fear. Traits are much more likely to be harmonious in their positive poles, but none of us are in our positive poles all the time. Strong negative poles can ruin relationships.

Aside from positive and negative poles, every pair of overleaves has a particular chemistry. Attraction due to overleaves is less clear-cut but they can be a factor.

Especially with opposite overleaves (those on the same axis), there could be either attraction or repulsion depending on whether we see the other person as balancing our strengths with different strengths or as being weak where he "should" be strong. This can also be the case between the neutral overleaves and any of the others.

A busy person with a goal of *growth*, for example, may find relief and relaxation with someone in *flow*, the neutral goal, and the person in flow may be stimulated by a partner in growth. However, they might also judge each other, especially in the negative poles. The person in growth might judge the person in flow as being lazy; the laid-back person in flow might judge the overwhelmed person in growth as being driven. There can be a similar dynamic between a person in growth and someone with the opposite goal, *reevaluation*, in which a person seeks a simple, more inward life and tends to be unambitious.

Someone with a goal of *discrimination* may be attracted to the warm openness of someone in the opposite, *acceptance*; however, the person in acceptance may flinch at the discriminator's rejections, especially if he tends to be in the negative pole.

Even people with the same overleaves could either attract or repel, having a comforting similarity or pushing each other's buttons, depending on the individuals. I could imagine two people who have the attitude of cynic (perhaps the most difficult overleaf) either getting along famously—spitting tobacco and commiserating about how the world has gone to hell—or feuding bitterly. And they may go back and forth between the two extremes.

I enjoy being with others who, like myself, have a goal of acceptance. However, since I can be too much in my head, I find it refreshing to be with people in the emotional center and passion mode to balance my dry intellectual center and observation mode.

As with the other overleaves, *chief obstacle* combinations could go either way in terms of attraction, although they are more likely to repel, especially if they're strong, since by definition they're negative. In the old school, some arrogance (of either the chief obstacle variety or just testosterone-driven overconfidence) was considered attractive in men, and some self-deprecation attractive in women. An arrogant person may like it that someone in self-deprecation isn't threatening, and his apparent confidence may reassure her; however, his criticisms can exacerbate her sense of inadequacy. Two people greedy for the same things might align in a relationship, and two people in self-destruction might share vices. However, two people in strong arrogance or impatience can enrage each other, and two people in stubbornness easily get into stalemates. An impatient person will tend to become impatient with a martyr, making him feel more martyred. If someone in impatience pushes someone in stubbornness, the latter will likely dig in her heels. And so forth. In any case, it's not a good idea to get into a relationship based on chief obstacles since they are fear-based.

Incidentally, those in stubbornness may find many excuses not to leave a bad relationship, dragging out the process ad nauseam. Those in impatience may not give a relationship a full chance before they're "outa here."

8 ♡ KARMA

When we are near someone with whom we have incomplete karma, we may start to buzz with an excitement that is similar to that of attraction and is often confused for it if the person is of the right gender, age, and look. People who are inexorably drawn into an abusive relationship and can't seem to leave are sometimes repaying a karmic debt. When the debt is repaid, the excitement goes flat, the person "returns to his senses," and can then leave the relationship, often wondering at that point what he ever saw in the other person.

True attraction delights. Completing a negative karma doesn't feel good but it is a relief, especially at the end of it. It discharges energy rather than builds it. Sometimes repaying a karmic debt or allowing one to be repaid to us is necessary to allow us to move on to a better relationship.

9 ♡ ASTROLOGY

Astrology, like the Michael teachings, is a system that can help explain attraction. It is more likely to reflect factors covered here than to introduce entirely new ones but it can offer much valuable information. If you have full birth information on yourself and a prospective mate, there are sites that will analyze how your charts intersect. For more nuance, though, you'll want a reading from a professional astrologer.

I am a Libra with a Scorpio ascendant. It is uncanny how all my life, I've been attracted, both romantically and as friends, to people whose birthdays are between November 4–18. In addition, I'm especially comfortable with fellow Libras. Other people report astrological patterns of attraction as well.

10 ♡ VIBRATIONAL RESONANCE

We each vibrate at a particular level based on the inner work we've done to refine and purify our energy, both in this lifetime and in past lifetimes. It is not directly related to soul age and has nothing to do with frequency on the Michael chart. It's the quality of love, truth, and beauty we emanate. A lot of baggage such as stored anger or fear, or a lot of limiting beliefs, brings down this quality.

I once met Louise Hay at a book convention. Because it wasn't a New Age event, she was standing alone rather than being mobbed by fans. I spoke to her for a moment to thank her for her work. Her outer style was a bit cool and distant, probably developed over the years for protection. However, I've never felt such a high-frequency energy field. Standing next to her was like being at the ocean, bathed in negative ions and fresh oxygen. She had obviously purified her thoughts and feelings to a high degree, giving her a powerfully loving presence. I imagine that many gurus feel like this, too. It must have been extraordinary to be in the presence of someone like Jesus or the Buddha, even before the *infinite soul* (a representative of a high plane) entered.

I know some mature souls whose vibration feels much higher than that of some old souls. Our vibration isn't directly related to soul age because, although having a higher soul age might give us more potential in this regard, it's the work we do that actualizes that potential. We go through cycles of accumulating experience and then processing it. Even a seventh-level old soul who was abused as a child and still harbors anger and fear will not shine like he would if those things were faced and healed. Any unwillingness to examine issues or lack of consistent integrity lowers one's vibration and are not directly related to soul age.

Like attracts like. It's uncomfortable to be around someone long-term who vibrates at a different level. If someone who is interested in you is vibrating at a significantly lower vibration than you are, he will either be drawn to do the work to raise his vibration or he will separate from you. More often, people choose separation rather than doing the hard work of facing their "stuff."

I would imagine that someone like Louise Hay would have difficulty finding a mate since there are few people who vibrate at her level. When you add that to all the other things we need for a relationship to work, it can be like finding a needle in a haystack.

Many of my clients and friends, male and female, straight and gay, are in this predicament. It's not hopeless but it can take a lot of patience to find a good match. There are always compromises in relationships—no one is perfect or has everything we are looking for. However, compromising too much on vibrational clarity isn't likely to end well. And if we want to be with someone who has a high vibration, we must also develop and maintain our own, living in integrity, facing our issues, and releasing our anger and fear.

11 ♡ CELIBACY AND UNION

The path of spiritual evolution that we're all on contains a series of separations and reunifications. When we first emerge into the dimensional universe from the *Tao* (the ground of all being), we fragment into individual souls, which separate further into various reincarnational personalities, each with a multitude of parallel selves that contain myriad subpersonalities. This fragmentation allows for a multiplication of experience. It is like light passing through a series of prisms. These parts of self were always there as potential, just as all colors are potential in light, and countless children are potential in sperm and eggs. The universe is about manifesting potential and seeing where it leads. As individuations or *sparks* of the Tao, we mature through having experiences. As we process them, we work our way back into full union with the Tao through smaller unions along the way. When we complete our journey and are wholly reassimilated into the Tao, we will have contributed a new level of development and expansion to it.

We tend to think of sex as only a physical thing. However, sex is our physical body's way of experiencing the union that everything in the universe seeks. Souls on higher planes merge their energies in increasingly complex and powerful ways. There is no creation without the union of

11 CELIBACY AND UNION

opposites: masculine and feminine, positive and negative (as in magnetic charges), active and passive, etc. Physical union may or may not result in the creation of new physical life, but all union creates new energies.

When we come into union with others in a clean, centered way, there is a clean creation. The more powerful the union, the more substantial the creation. This applies not only to physical sex but to any coming together. Power, obviously, can be misused, and many people are afraid of it for that reason. Without power, however, there is no evolution. As we work with what we can handle well, our skill grows. Loving relationships are bound to bring up unresolved issues but they can also provide a means for healing them.

The physical plane is the elementary school of union, and for us, sex can be the apogee of that. The tantric tradition teaches how to include mental, emotional, and spiritual union in sexual union, and those who come together in deep love may experience that intuitively. There's nothing wrong with sex that is mainly physical gratification but when sex includes higher unions as well, it is richer.

Many religions glorify celibacy and teach people to be ashamed of their attractions, but without attractions, there would be no unions. Union with God or the All-That-Is doesn't preclude union with people; in fact, when union with people is adequately free of mental/emotional baggage, it is a vehicle for union with God—not the only one, but a valid one, and for most people, the most powerful.

Tantra also teaches that energy is lost through ejaculation and that men should instead send sexual energy up their spine. Some people believe that energy expended sexually is not available for spiritual growth or creativity. However, as Michael said in *Messages from Michael* by Chelsea Quinn Yarbro, there's little loss of energy in sex when it's free of baggage. Also, doctors say that about three ejaculations per week are helpful for a healthy prostate. Perhaps men could beneficially use tantric non-ejaculatory techniques in addition to rather than in place of regular sexual activities—finding balance in all things is a key to life. Too little and too much are equally detrimental. Some people are addicted to sex, which does lead to a loss of energy. Sex addictions can be similar to food addictions, which are often the result of a junk food diet that leaves people's needs unsatisfied, causing them to seek more. The solution may be to increase quality.

It's also been scientifically validated that a good sex life makes the body healthier. Surely more energy is lost in repressing natural desires and living with unfulfilled needs than through balanced sex, although temporary celibacy can help one detach from unhealthy patterns. If someone

11 CELIBACY AND UNION

working on his spiritual growth feels that he's not yet capable of staying clear while in a relationship, celibacy might be like the neutral gear allowing him to shift to a higher gear. Some people need to be alone for a time so that they don't have to deal with another person's issues while they're healing their own and growing into themselves. Sometimes, though, they become set in patterns and have a difficult time breaking out of them once the need to be alone is no longer there.

Long-term celibacy can be someone's authentic path. When that is the case, it is likely to be fairly easy. Shame about sexuality or running from the challenges of relationships are not healthy reasons for celibacy.

Eastern philosophies teach the value of non-attachment and freedom from desire. Most healthy bodies have sexual attractions, just as they have hunger for food and thirst for drink. Freedom from desire doesn't mean that one doesn't have desires—that's not possible. It means not being controlled by them, being at peace in the present moment and not needing anything external in order to be happy. As we evolve, we have more self-control and make choices based on the whole picture rather than momentary urges. From non-attachment (different from detachment), we can enjoy sex or anything else that naturally flows in our lives without tightly holding on to it or making it more (or less) than it is.

The child-molestation scandal in the Catholic Church points to the distortions that can arise from repressing natural drives. There have also been many sex scandals with gurus who claimed to be celibate who weren't, some of whom abused their position and took advantage of followers.

In addition to misunderstanding freedom from desire, religious celibacy requirements derive in part from a dualistic belief that you can't have both God and sex, as if they were separate. Also, they have to do with religions controlling their workforce and ensuring that its labors financially accrue to them rather than to families. Gay sex between monks, priests, and nuns has actually been common and quietly tolerated throughout much of history since it doesn't lead to babies.

Throughout most of human history, people mated shortly after adolescence began. The relatively recent expectation that "good" teenagers won't be sexually active is unrealistic and even cruel, considering that it's the body's time of greatest desire. Of course, no one should be pushed to have sex before he or she ready, but providing education and a safe environment for first sexual encounters, allowing them to be the sweet experiences they can be, would be a great gift and would likely reduce the acting out teenagers do.

Celibacy for unmarried people (and monogamy after marriage) may have made some theoretical sense in the past in that it avoided unwanted

11 CELIBACY AND UNION

babies, helped ensure that children would have both parents on hand, and stemmed the spread of sexually transmitted diseases. However, despite constant shaming and fierce restraints on women, biology has often won out. Today, with modern medicine and contraceptives, the case for celibacy and monogamy is weaker. Even in the past, it would have been more sensible and effective to simply teach young people how to avoid pregnancy. There are fewer unwanted pregnancies among teens who have had sex education.

Shame about natural functions leads to many distortions that spill over into all parts of society. A *New York Times* Op-Ed, "The Sexual Misery of the Arab World," demonstrates the link between repression and political ills. It stands to reason, for instance, that frustrated, unhappy people are more likely to go to war or commit terrorism. Maturing into a healthy, uncharged view of sex yields many benefits.

Sex brings a merging of energies, and it may be unwise to have sex with someone whose energy we don't like since we'll end up carrying it around for a few days. The more intense the sex, the more true this is. So it's a good idea to have a healthy respect for its power. On the other hand, sex is a biological need; burdening it too much with the weight of morality warps it. Like anything else, it can be used irresponsibly or to harm others, but of itself it is neutral. As long as it's consensual and those involved take responsibility for their choices, it is not a moral issue. No government has a right to regulate harmless consensual behavior between adults, and the age of consent should probably be lowered to 14 or so as it is in Hawaii (it's 16-18 in most states). How unjust that in some states, a 19-year-old dating a 17-year-old can be charged with statutory rape.

Those who don't have a satisfying sex life and who would like one (which is probably the majority) are understandably frustrated. Even more basic is the human need for touch, which obviously sex provides. It's been found that babies who aren't touched will die. Some African tribes view the Western tradition of having children sleep alone in their own bed as child abuse. You can observe how children often want to get into bed with their parents. And adults who aren't touched have more health problems. We live in a society in which many children aren't breast-fed and grow up starved for touch, and "touchy-feely" is an epithet.

On the other hand, we won't die if we don't have sex, even if it feels that way at times. Our sex drive is related to our survival instinct. If we're feeling panicked because of the lack of a partner, it's largely because our body believes that if we don't have sex and reproduce, the whole human race will die out. Obviously, that's not going to happen, so we can reassure our body consciousness and

11 CELIBACY AND UNION

help calm it down. It's in our interests to relax our body; for one thing, being too needy generally isn't attractive.

If our needs aren't being met, we can still work with union in the ways that are available to us until we find an appropriate partner. One is to be a good lover to ourselves when masturbating. Another is to open our hearts to union with nature. Through meditation, we can open to union with the universe. Artistic and other creativity can be an outlet for some of our sexual energies.

On a more practical level, many of us who are seeking mates aren't putting ourselves out there enough, making it harder for potential mates to find us. There's also often inner work to be done to release blocks such as the famous fear of intimacy—it's important to have a clear intent and not send out mixed messages. After we've done all the work that we know how to do, both inner and outer, it then just might be a matter of being patient and letting go.

Some people have found their mate after deeply letting go of wanting one (not the same as giving up or becoming resigned) and becoming peaceful with being single. It's similar to what happens with some couples who desperately want to become pregnant but finally accept their situation and adopt; surprisingly often, they then get pregnant. In both cases, wanting something too much stood as a block to having it, perhaps because so much of their energy was focusing on the lack. Paradoxically, relaxing with how things are gives us more power to create change.

We each have spirit guides working behind the scenes to help us carry out our life plan. They do the best they can to bring us potential mates when we seek one but we humans often don't listen to our spiritual impulses—from our guides' point of view, it can be like herding cats. Still, spirit is persistent. If our path is to be in a happy mate relationship, we probably eventually will be as long as we stay responsive to our intuition, keep doing our inner work, and put ourselves out there.

PART II
PSYCHOLOGICAL FACTORS IN ATTRACTION

12 ♡ FINDING BALANCE

When we cut ourselves off from any part of ourselves, we then long for it. For example, if we've denied our body, we long to feel connected with it and are likely to be highly attracted to people who are strongly physical. It may look like they have something unattainable to us, such as physical self-confidence or athleticism, but what we long for is actually something available within ourselves, a potential we are called to actualize. If it weren't our potential, we probably wouldn't long for it—it wouldn't even be on our radar. The shadow of such attraction is judgment and rejection, due to the reasons we denied our body in the first place—we may, for example, believe that the body is dirty or sinful. Denial sets up a polarity, and attraction can flip-flop with rejection. When we own and integrate our body, that kind of attraction fades along with the rejection.

12 FINDING BALANCE

People who repress their emotions tend to attract partners who are overemotional, or who at least become overemotional in the relationship in an unconscious attempt to balance it. In many couples, the feminine partner carries not only her own emotions but those of her partner, who leaves her the job out of his unwillingness to feel his. However, since he's denying his own emotions, he also denies hers, and may accuse her of being a "hysterical female." Sometimes, she leaves him the job of carrying her intellect if she hasn't developed it, perhaps because she has been too busy carrying all the emotions in the relationship. In this way, natural strengths are exaggerated, and relationships become excessively polarized. Some people are more emotional and some, more intellectual or physical, but we all need to think, feel and act for ourselves if we are to be whole.

If we're cut off from our creativity and that's an important part of who we are, then someone who is wildly creative will be compelling. If we worship that person, putting him on a pedestal, we might be really expressing how much we long to express our own creativity. We may think that we don't have much but that's probably not the case.

If our masculine or feminine side is underdeveloped, we may be attracted to someone in whom that side is overdeveloped at the expense of the opposite energy. This can be the case whether we're male or female and whether our soul is higher in male or female energy. We all have at least some of both energies and need free access to both in order to be in balance. The place of balance is different for each person—most of us won't be in our male and female energies exactly half the time—but being able to use both energies when needed allows us to feel whole. When we're in balance, we're still attracted to our opposite but it doesn't come from a place of trying to get something we think we don't have. Rather, when both do what comes naturally, they complement. [For some fascinating, original thinking on this, see http://deida.info.]

There are elements of projection in most relationships. We project both the gifts we long for and deny, which can result in idolizing the other person, and the traits we judge and deny in ourselves, which usually results in fault-finding. In either case, we are unable to see the other person for who he is. Relationships based more on projection than on real connection are bound to fail; where there is illusion, disillusionment comes sooner or later. The answer is taking responsibility for being who we want to be and dealing with our own issues, revealing ourselves as we are and seeing our partner fairly. What our partner does is up to her—we cannot make someone see us clearly. However, if we are revealing ourselves and someone consistently still doesn't see us, she's not good mate material for us.

12 FINDING BALANCE

Developing any part of ourselves makes that part more attractive. Athletes make their body more attractive by putting energy and therefore consciousness (light) into it. The shape and tone they develop are beautiful, but they are in part a result of increased physical consciousness. People who are healthy and vigorous have a kind of light in their eyes that demonstrates that. Mental, emotional, and spiritual development likewise make those aspects of self shinier and more attractive. Rarely are all levels of self developed equally, and that's not necessarily a person's path—many of us specialize in one area of development in a given lifetime—but it's helpful to attain as much balance as possible.

It's easy to rest on our strengths and it takes discipline to develop our weaker areas, but increased balance has many rewards: it makes everything we do more efficient (it's easier to think clearly, for example, if we're physically active) and helps us feel more whole. It also makes us attractive in more ways and, therefore, to more people. Athletes might find balance by reading or making music. An intellectual can benefit from exercising or meditating.

13 ♡ PARENTS

TAKING RESPONSIBLILITY

Unresolved issues with our parents can result in unhealthy attractions and relationship dynamics. In working through wounds about what our parents didn't give us, it's good to keep in mind that no one can give what he doesn't have. Most parents love in the ways they know how. Acknowledging the truth about the way we were parented is helpful, but blaming our parents for where we are now is not; once we're adults, we are responsible for ourselves. Being responsible is not the same as blaming ourselves, either—it simply means that we accept how things are as a starting point, and then roll up our sleeves and do something about them.

This is not to suggest that we should gloss over painful feelings—they need to be acknowledged, felt, and loved in order to be healed. Also, this doesn't let parents off the hook if they were abusive or neglectful—we're each responsible for our acts even when we are ignorant. However, the ultimate solution to our parents' shortcomings is to find within what was lacking. For example, if our parents didn't believe in us, we can believe in ourselves now. One of the primary ways we grow is by overcoming the limitations into which we were born.

13 PARENTS

Mainstream psychology, lacking understanding of the soul, is quick to attribute most personality defects to bad parenting. That places an undue burden of fear and guilt on parents. Knowledge of past lives makes it clear that parenting is only part of the picture. After undergoing past-life therapy, I saw that I'd brought many of my issues with me into this lifetime. Seeing this helped me become more forgiving of my parents.

WE CHOSE OUR PARENTS

There are many possible reasons why we as souls might choose particular parents (and why they might choose us to be their children). Sometimes, they are relatively unimportant in the scheme of our life—they just provided an appropriate body and circumstance. More often, they are highly significant. For example, we may choose them because of karma or other major life issues we need to work out.

Typically, we make an agreement with the soul of one parent to be its child. The other parent, who may not have been on the scene when the agreement was made, comes along as part of the package. A couple who has more than one child generally alternates between fulfilling the mother's and father's child agreements. However, which soul incarnates into a particular infant is negotiable and plans can change at the last minute as circumstances shift. Suppose that before a birth, the parents decide to divorce. The soul slated to incarnate may not want to take on that situation, opening the way for another soul who was also interested in that body. Just as parents usually have more than one child agreement, souls planning to incarnate usually make agreements with more than one potential parent. If we were hoping to be the child of someone who decided not to have children, for example, we go to plan B.

The parent with whom we have our child agreement is likely to be particularly catalytic for us, and it's not necessarily the one we like better or feel closer to. This parent can be especially influential on our attractions and the patterns we repeat. However, he or she is often not so much the cause of our issues but a trigger for latent ones that we carry from past lives. We may choose a parent precisely because he or she is likely to bring forward difficult issues that we want to try to resolve.

FATHER AND MOTHER GOD

Our psyche operates on symbols. When we're children, our parents represent the masculine and feminine aspects of God (or the universe) to us. They are the Source for us, and we want them to be perfect (just as we want God to be perfect) so that we can feel safe in relying on them to provide for us and show us the way to be. The decreasing stability of family and religion in our society is partly responsible for the ascendancy of our worship of movie stars, royalty, and other celebrities. The child in each of us has an inborn need for heroes to emulate, and if we can't find them at home or church, we look elsewhere. Unfortunately, what we find is usually pretty shallow.

As we mature spiritually, we ourselves become a hero, a representative of Father/Mother God, embodying traits such as integrity and compassion. Our need for external symbols of it decreases as we manifest our soul and therefore connect with God (the whole) directly. Because role models have been successfully fulfilling their function for us, they become less needed, although there are always higher levels to attain—we can continue to find inspiration in the strengths that others embody. If we've been hung up on our parents, it's then easier to release them. We no longer need to follow the scripts they imprinted on us. However, nobody is fully mature in all areas—we all have pockets of unhealed emotions that keep us partly stuck in the past. This is illustrated when powerful adults visit their parents and become twelve-year-olds again. Such experiences show us what we still need to work on in order to experience more wholeness.

The idealized loving nuclear family has always been far less common than nostalgia would indicate, even when the divorce rate was lower. Although a warm, close-knit family is wonderful, not having that can be more growthful—it is the irritating sand in oysters that makes pearls grow. People from *Leave It to Beaver* families may not develop the depth they otherwise might because they don't have to. There's an archetype of the "wounded healer"—those of us who went through rough childhoods may have met the challenges by accessing resources we can then use to more effectively help others. That said, there's no need to manufacture extra challenges for children to toughen them up—the world provides enough. A loving home can help create a solid foundation of self-esteem and life skills to help deal with a difficult world. If a soul hungers for growth and deepening, it will attract the necessary tools, whatever they may be.

PICTURES OF REALITY

Our pictures of reality are extremely powerful; we create our life from them. Observing our life gives us the opportunity to examine our pictures and change them if we don't like what we've created.

Without accurate pictures of what a truly loving and happy life can look like, we cannot create that reality. Perhaps the world's biggest problem is a lack of vision. We cannot have peace, freedom, or anything else we long for if we cannot specifically envision it. Many people simply have no idea what a mature expression of love looks like, so they have no way to experience it. We all long to share love, but faulty notions about it can sabotage it. For example, if our parents bickered constantly, that

13 PARENTS

may be part of our picture of relationships. Becoming conscious of our pictures gives us the ability to change them.

Our pictures of reality develop from the conclusions we've drawn about our experiences over many lifetimes. In addition, we also take on our family's energies, which include pictures that can go back several generations. These may coincide with our past-life pictures, and it's possible we even incarnated in our family in previous lifetimes.

Simply being aware of our pictures is a powerful first step in changing them. Deliberately holding new pictures when the old ones come up can gradually erase them. Processes such as the brilliant Family Constellations workshop can clear family pictures; past-life therapy can help us release pictures formed from traumas before this lifetime.

It is disorienting when reality doesn't match our pictures. For example, if someone's picture is that men are abusive because her father was, and she gets involved with a man who is kind to her, it can be confusing. To make reality match her picture, she may unconsciously manipulate him in order to try to get him to be abusive, or she may turn off her attraction to him and move on until she finds someone who fits her picture. Or, she may wake up and change her picture. With positive, healthy pictures of reality, we are unlikely to end up in abusive relationships.

As children, our parents are our role models for what it is to be a man or woman. We desperately want to be able to admire them and grow up to be like them. We also want to view them as ideal mates. Therefore, we tend to carry their pictures of reality. Even if, as adults, we can see that their pictures were distorted in various ways, our subconscious may still hold them and be creating our reality accordingly.

It is often said that someone married her father or mother. If we're fortunate, we are attracted to someone like one of our parents simply because he or she was a great role model. As the old song goes, "I want a girl just like the girl who married dear old dad." We can also, however, attract mates who are like the parent with whom we're more unresolved if there were major issues, in an attempt to work them out. A friend who has been unsuccessfully trying to extricate himself from his controlling mother all his life still ended up with a long-term partner much like her (and who got along with her famously).

INCOMPLETION

The Oedipus complex is not universal but it is fairly common in our society when a child feels he has to compete with one parent for the other's affections because the parent is unwilling to share his spouse. A pattern of competition can repeat for generations since children who feel deprived of adequate love may grow up not wanting to share their spouse with their own children. This is another reason someone may "marry his mother" or father—he is still trying to get what he didn't get as a child.

There can be a need to cut the "apron strings" with a parent (or both parents). The Michael teachings describe a life's seven *internal monads* or passages. The third occurs around the age of eighteen when we start to establish independence from our family. If this doesn't occur in a healthy way, there's likely to be problems in relationships, or an inability to commit to a mate at all. If a parent has died, loving a mate can seem like a betrayal of her memory, as if it means we no longer love her. Finding a sense of completion and letting go can be more difficult when a parent has passed, but we can still communicate spiritually with deceased loved ones. Those on the other side want resolution as much as we do.

TEMPLATES

We sometimes unconsciously follow templates we observed in our parents. A man I know married a woman who resembled his mother. His parents had divorced when his father was forty, and when he turned forty, he divorced his wife. It was as if he looked at his inner watch and said, "It's time to get divorced." The problems he cited seemed fixable, more like rationalizations for following the script than real reasons. Many subsequent events also eerily paralleled those of his childhood. For example, his second wife unexpectedly had to raise his children from his first marriage, just as his stepmother had. Repeating these patterns was an unconscious way of exploring his unresolved issues; he re-experienced those events from the other side, as father rather than son. Had he been more conscious of the issues, he might not have needed to act them out.

A friend first married when she was past forty, just like her father, whom she adored. Both her father and husband had the same soul type and were in similar businesses. Her relationship with her mother was extremely problematic but after years of therapy, she managed not to marry someone like her—she had worked it out enough so that she did not have to reenact those dynamics. Instead, she both emulated and "married her father," which for her was a positive thing.

Some people even die at the same age as their dominant parent because they don't feel it would right to live longer than she did, or because their picture is that that's the right time to die. Such patterns can be hidden under the guise of apparently hereditary diseases.

A client of mine had three long-term relationships that followed a template established by her father. He had been pretty kindly before her mother died when she was a child. After that, he went off the deep end and became abusive. Similarly, the three mates were loving until she had given up other options to be with them; then they turned abusive and irrational. Her picture of reality drew those who would naturally play the part that matched her picture, and she may have unconsciously helped create their behavior as well. She did have one happy relationship, but after a few years, he came to feel like a brother to her. Perhaps she turned off her attraction because he was not following the script—he remained kind.

Most of us have some repeating patterns in our life, situations we somehow manage to recreate over and over again in spite of our best intentions. Observing and taking responsibility for them can help us shift our beliefs and energies, and thus create a new reality.

14 ♡ RESOLVING THE PAST

Our past is our past whether in this lifetime, past lifetimes, or even previous planetary cycles. We are always seeking to work out unresolved issues. Having experiences is the raw material of growth. As we process them, we become more conscious of what we learned and transform our wounds into strengths—our growth becomes more fully realized. Anything we do in life may be used for resolving issues.

There are many reasons people might be drawn to a particular fetish or sexual practice, but frequently there is a desire to resolve issues from the past. People who are into the dungeon scene, for example, may be trying to heal past-life imprisonment experiences as either victim, victimizer, or both.

The more traumatic an experience was, the more likely it is to be carried forward into future lifetimes until it is resolved. Although being whipped for punishment is rare in the modern Western world, whipping still holds some fascination in fetish circles, in part due to past-life memories from when it was more common. Furthermore, if a person numbed himself to survive the ordeal, he may only be able to experience sexual (and other) feelings under great intensity such as whipping or other pain because subtlety doesn't register when we're numb. The

14 RESOLVING THE PAST

fetish keeps drawing him back to the trauma in an unconscious effort to heal it. Acting out the fetish safely with boundaries he controls can be a way of healing the wound, gradually taking the charge out of it, releasing fear, anger, confusion, or whatever other emotions it carries.

As we become more self-aware, easier and more efficient methods of healing the past become available to us. At first, acting out trauma might be useful to bring it to the surface and impress upon us just what we're dealing with if we'd buried it, but working with it directly without acting it out can be more effective and less stressful. Today, there are many fast and powerful psychospiritual techniques. Peter Levine's books including *Waking the Tiger* are about healing trauma through accessing the body's wisdom. Past-life regression can be especially useful when examining the current lifetime doesn't yield results. Whatever technique is used, the key is to bring consciousness to what has been unconscious. Consciousness brings light and movement to what was dark and stuck. All healing involves an expansion of consciousness. Whenever we're able to bring consciousness directly to bear, healing is much faster. Advanced students are sometimes able to go directly into the energy that holds a pattern, releasing and healing it without a lot of analysis or expression, simply by consciously being with it in love.

For example, someone might carry frozen energy containing fear and anger as a result of having been raped in either the present or a past life. In meditation, she could ask her body to "light up" where she is holding the dysfunctional pattern (in her genitals, for instance). Then, by directly feeling and enfolding it, and staying with it as it responds to her awareness, it may clear. She may get pictures of what happened, or she may simply be aware of changing sensations. If her meditation is not able to fully clear what she's holding, she could try it again later. At a minimum, such work would help other forms of therapy be more effective. Some imprints go so deep that no matter how much good work we do, we may not entirely erase them. This is where self-acceptance comes in.

Our subconscious operates in part through associating things that seem related; that is a principle behind fetishes. If, for example, an article of clothing was present at a time of strong arousal, especially in our youth, it may become sexualized so that it then becomes an instrument of future arousal.

According to studies, people who were spanked as children are more likely to be aroused by being spanked when having sex. Especially if they were spanked by a parent who showed them little other attention, they might equate being spanked with love.

14 RESOLVING THE PAST

People exploring dualities often eventually switch roles as a means of finding balance. Dominant people may become submissive, hypermasculine people might explore hyperfemininity, or vice versa. When they thoroughly learn the lessons of both sides, they can balance and integrate them internally, no longer needing to experience either extreme in a negative, distorted way.

In the Michael teachings, this is illustrated in the goals of *dominance* and *submission*. Someone with a goal of dominance is naturally more dominant. However, she may *slide* or temporarily move to the opposite goal, submission. A person who is submissive in a healthy way, with self-esteem, might find genuine joy in playing a supportive role. The positive pole of submission is *devotion* (the negative is *subservience*). Also, those with the role of king are naturally more dominant than servers, although there are servers with a goal of dominance and kings with a goal of submission, which mixes things up a bit.

Acting out fantasies sometimes reveals that the reality isn't as exciting as the fantasy, releasing some of the charge around them. At the same time, there's nothing wrong with role-playing or other games to "spice up" sex. The expression roles, artisans and sages, especially tend to enjoy playing in this way. It's no coincidence that the second chakra is said to govern both sexuality and creativity. Sex that loses creativity and spontaneity also tends to lose its intensity.

Any form of sexual expression can introduce variety and establish a framework for relating. However, the real power and satisfaction come from connecting fully soul to soul in the moment, what Michael calls *essence contact*; if one is focused on the form or is just replaying the past, the experience is not likely to be deeply satisfying.

PART III
PHYSICAL FACTORS IN ATTRACTION

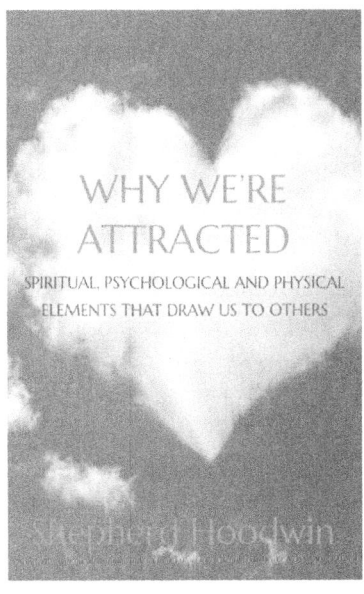

15 ♡ BODY-TYPE ATTRACTION

Body types are a highly significant factor in physical attraction. This elegantly symmetrical system is part of both the Michael and Gurdjieff teachings, and has been taught throughout history in various esoteric schools. [I go into more detail on them in *Journey of Your Soul*. *Body Types* by Joel Friedlander is entirely devoted to them.] This information, like much of what is provided in this book, will be more meaningful if you have your body types channeled or are able to identify them through study.

Body types are physical and psychological traits stemming from the influences of celestial bodies on our physical bodies. There are loose, indirect correlations between our body types and astrological influences.

We each combine two to four body types influences. For example, my body is 53% lunar, 36% martial, and 11% venusian. The opposites of each of our types can contribute to body-type attraction. I have maximum body-type attraction with someone who has 53% saturnian, 36% venusian, and 11% martial. However, there is body-type attraction whenever any significant amount of opposite influences are present.

Below are the seven major body types, followed by their:

15 BODY-TYPE ATTRACTION

- Positive and negative poles (summaries of how they manifest at their best and worst)
- Structure: active or passive, positive or negative charge, and masculine, feminine, or androgynous, discussed below
- Physical traits
- Psychological traits, and
- Examples, both human and cartoon.

Each opposite pair shares the same axis (fundamental quality): inspiration, expression, action, and assimilation.

The illustrations are used by permission from *Michael—The Basic Teachings*.

INSPIRATION

LUNAR
+ Luminous – Pallid
Passive, negative, and feminine
Pale, "baby fat," round-faced
Calm, introspective, mathematical
Andy Warhol, Emily Dickenson; Pillsbury Doughboy

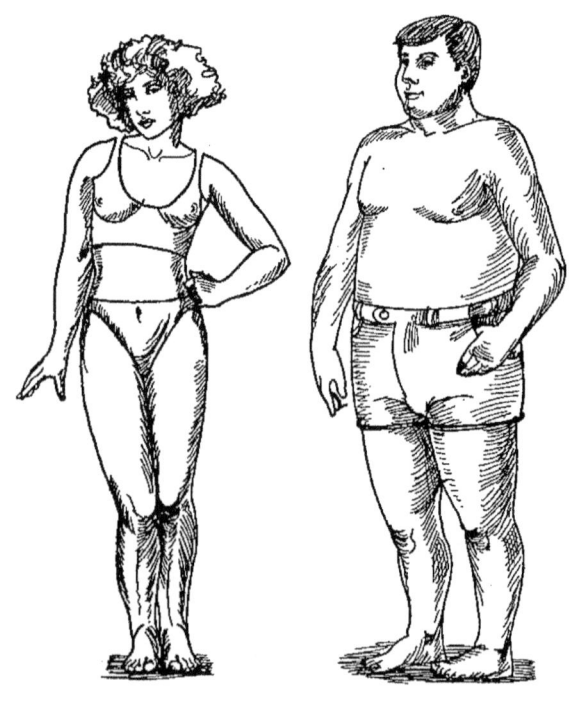

15 BODY-TYPE ATTRACTION

SATURNIAN
+ Rugged – Gaunt
Active, positive, and masculine
Tall, strong bones, high forehead
Enduring, self- control, leadership
Sam Shepard, Vanessa Redgrave; Uncle Sam

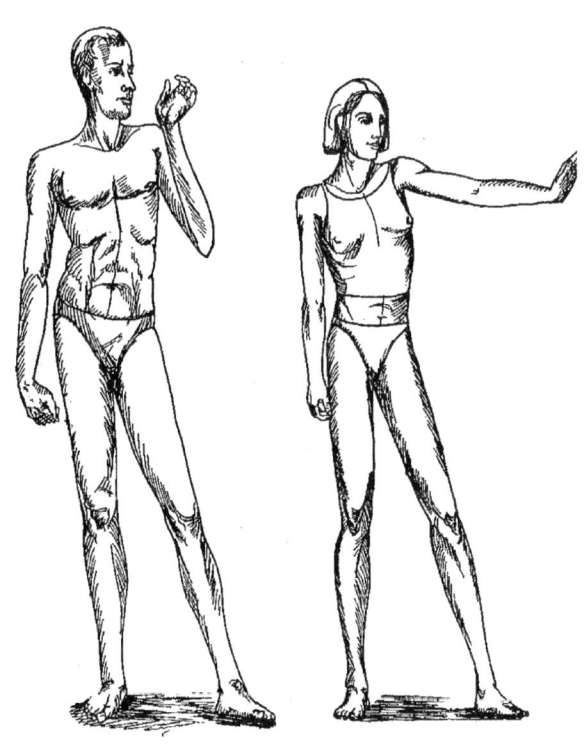

EXPRESSION

JOVIAL
+ Grand – Extravagant
Passive, positive, and masculine
Large, short, male-pattern baldness, wide-necked
Magnanimous, knowledgeable, pleasure-oriented
Orson Welles, Ethel Merman; Santa Claus

WITHOUT EXERCISE:

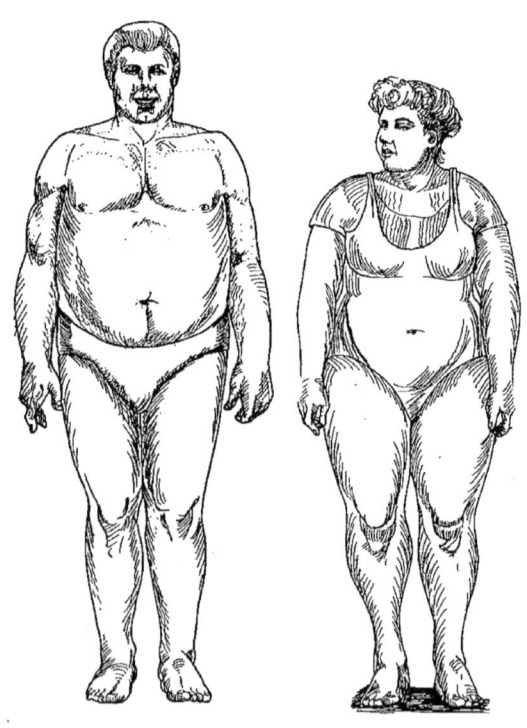

15 BODY-TYPE ATTRACTION

WITH EXERCISE:

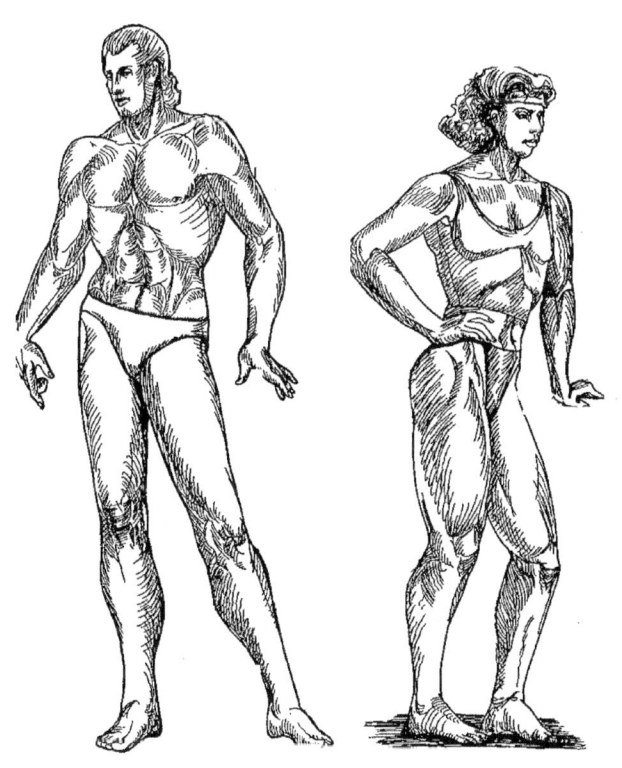

MERCURIAL

+ Agile – Frenetic
Active, negative, and feminine
Dark hair and eyes, slender, compact
Clever, quick, extroverted
George Gershwin, Debra Winger; Bugs Bunny

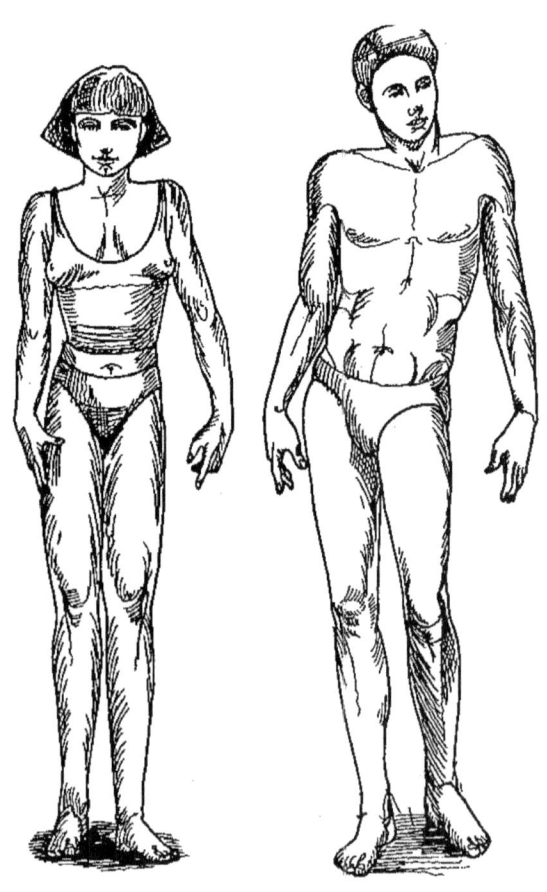

15 BODY-TYPE ATTRACTION

ACTION

VENUSIAN
+ Voluptuous – Obese
Passive, positive, and feminine
Dark and thick hair, olive skin, wide hands
Easygoing, sensual, loyal, nonjudgmental
Roseanne Barr, Tom Selleck; Jessica Rabbit

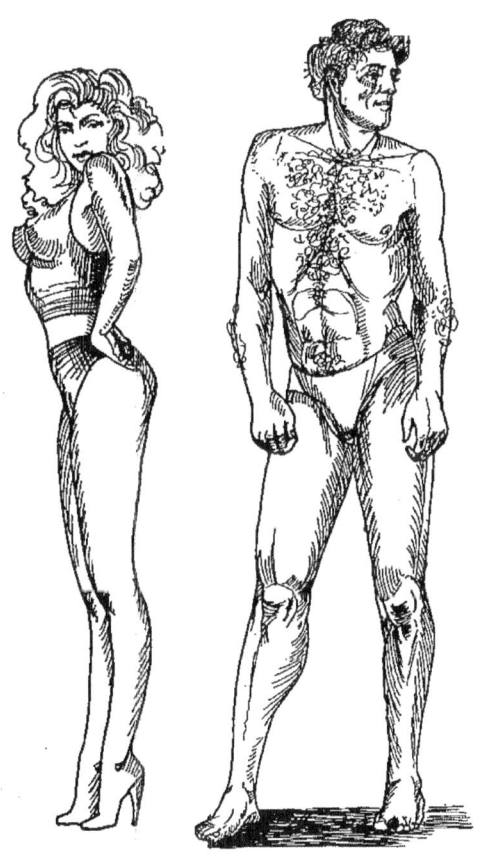

MARTIAL
+ Wiry – Muscle-bound
Active, negative, and masculine
Reddish coloring, sinewy, broad
Direct, decisive, volatile
Richard Burton, Katharine Hepburn; Yosemite Sam

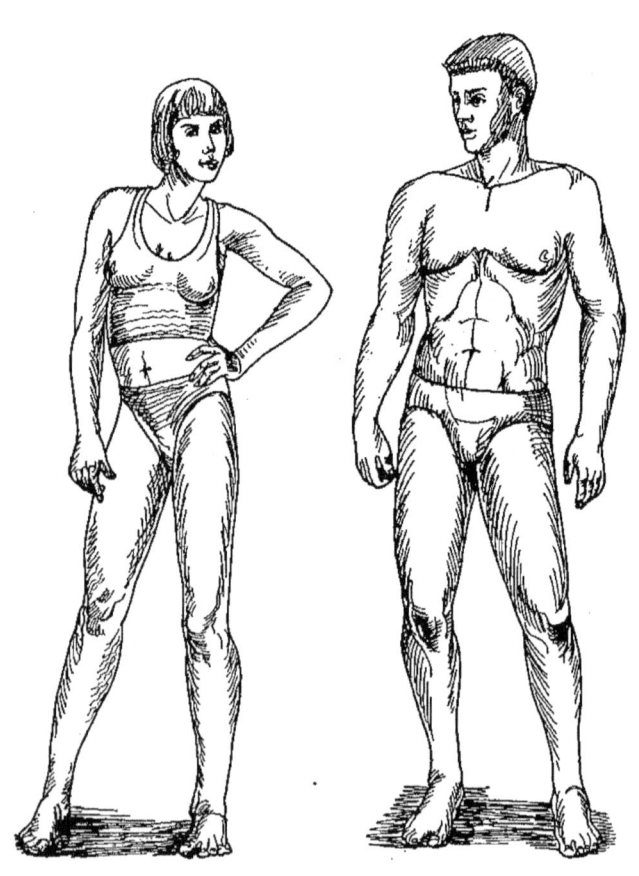

15 BODY-TYPE ATTRACTION

ASSIMILATION

SOLAR
+ Radiant – Ethereal
Active, positive, and androgynous
Delicate, slight, young-looking
Light-hearted, elegant, creative
Judy Garland, Michael Jackson; Peter Pan

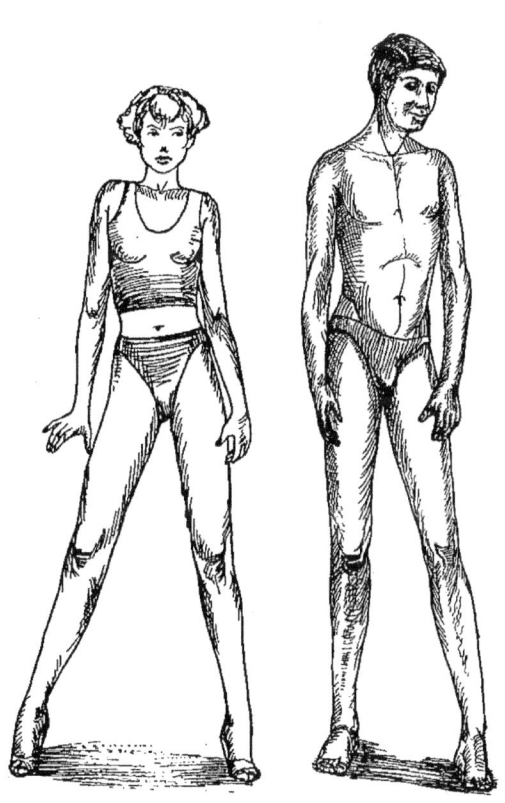

The personalities of the body types are evident in the way we use some of the terms in common parlance. The stereotype of the jolly fat person comes from the jovial body type, which tends to be large. Saturnians can be saturnine, i.e., sullen or stolid. Mercurials can be volatile and swift.

Body-type attraction between opposites can provide a "zing" in both sexual and non-sexual relationships—our bodies feel stimulated just by being together; they form a kind of electrical circuit. The pairs are opposite in three respects: active/passive, positive/negative (like the poles of a magnet), and masculine/feminine.

Active and passive refer to whether the body's tendency is to do or to be. Active bodies want to move; passive ones don't.

There are different degrees and kinds of activity and passivity. Lunar is the most passive, the calm epitome of being. Saturnian is the most active, the calm epitome of doing. Solar, the neutral type, is also active but lightly so: neither stolid (saturnian), wound-up (mercurial), nor explosive (martial). Jovials are passive in a gregarious way; venusians are passive in a sensual way.

The positive types are like the day: bright, optimistic, emphasizing the outer, and overlooking flaws. Solars are sunny, jovials are mirthful, venusians are warm, and saturnians have a can-do attitude.

15 BODY-TYPE ATTRACTION

The negative types are like the night: dark, pessimistic, emphasizing the inner, and noticing what needs correction. Negative doesn't refer to a bad attitude—it is simply one's natural slant on things. Lunars are sensitive and cool, mercurials can be sarcastic, and martials can be ill-tempered.

Feminine types receive. Lunars absorb strength, venusians soak up sensual stimulation, and mercurials take in energy (and can become wound up).

Masculine types emit. Saturnians exude leadership, martials discharge power (and can be explosive), and jovials release energy (sometimes dissipatively).

Solar is androgynous. The radiance of the solar type is simply present rather than forceful like the masculine types.

Since lunar is the most feminine type and saturnian is the most masculine, lunar men and saturnian women are more likely to be gay or bisexual than when the reverse is true, although body type is only one of many factors influencing sexual orientation.

Body-type attraction is not the same as thinking that someone is beautiful or handsome, or even that someone is our "type" (covered in the next chapter) or someone we'd want to be with. Beauty is, in part, a function of health, grooming, self-expression, and genetics. Human beings are hardwired to seek mates who seem likely to parent healthy babies. Cues include symmetrical features, as well as appearing healthy and fit.

Beauty is also, of course, in the eye of the beholder, which is influenced by our conditioning. Our image of beauty may relate to what advertising and the media in general promote. Our type may be someone who reminds us of one of our parents or an important earlier lover. Body-type attraction is more subtle—it is our body's fascination with its opposite. Simply sitting next to someone with an opposite body type can excite or stimulate our body, even if she's not our type or of interest as a sexual partner.

Incidentally, souls do not necessarily want to be in a body that would be considered handsome or beautiful. The soul craves a variety of experiences and lessons. Being beautiful might, for example, be considered a nuisance when the soul wishes to have a lifetime quietly observing life. Being good-looking may make sex more accessible but it doesn't necessarily make finding a good mate easier.

Body-type attraction can account for being drawn sexually to someone who isn't our type or doesn't conform to our image of what is good-looking. In addition, it can account for some of those "odd couple" relationships, such as a thin, small mercurial in relationship with a large jovial.

15 BODY-TYPE ATTRACTION

If someone is our type and there is also body-type attraction, that can be very compelling. One doesn't need to have body-type attraction to have a good sexual relationship, but it is an enhancement.

Not being someone's type can be a deal-breaker even with body-type attraction. One highly martial man I know is a fitness buff who isn't attracted to women who are even slightly overweight, yet venusian is his opposite and venusians put on weight relatively easily (think Oprah Winfrey), so he has always had trouble finding women to whom he's attracted.

Periodically, different body types come into fashion. Jovials were popular in the 1890s, as they were in the artist Reuben's time. The pale, moon-faced flapper look of the 1920s owed much to the lunar type. In the 1930s and 40s, mercurial's oval face and lithe body, exemplified by Fred Astaire, and pugnacious martial tough guys such as James Cagney, were popular. (Mars, the red planet, is also known as the god of war). The voluptuous sex symbols of the 1950s such as Marilyn Monroe and Elvis Presley embodied venusian influence (Venus is the mythological goddess of love). Twiggy's child-like solar look set the tone for the late 1960s. Since the 1980s, saturnians have been in fashion, so models tend to be tall, athletic, and thin. It's hard to believe today that often in the past, tall people were thought to look ungainly and thin people were considered bony.

Even today, not everyone shares our society's love of thinness: A very heavyset man I know visited an African tribe who asked him if he was royalty. People whose dominant parent was large or who feel themselves to be overly slight may be attracted to large partners. Sometimes it takes courage for a compact mercurial to "come out" about his attraction to large, even elephantine jovials, or a small, muscular martial about his love of voluptuous, even obese venusians.

Jovials and venusians are not necessarily overweight, but the passive types don't have an inborn need to be in frequent movement, and these two types especially like to indulge in the pleasures of good food and drink. Passive types also tend to have a slower metabolism so it can be difficult for them to lose weight. Active types can be overweight, too—psychological factors, such as a need for protection, can override body-type influences. In addition, health issues such as glandular problems or enforced sedentariness due to an injury can be a factor with anyone. If a person died of starvation in a past life vowing that it would never happen again, he may have a hard time controlling his subconscious need to put on excess weight. However, active types generally put on weight more slowly and take it off more easily than passive types.

15 BODY-TYPE ATTRACTION

Every type has pros and cons. For example, a soul who intends to be a writer might not want a highly active body type that can't bear to be "tied to a desk." There is usually enough wiggle room for our soul to create what it needs for that lifetime from the genetic raw material that parents provide.

Some body types repel: mercurial and martial, for example. Both are negative and active, but they function differently: mercurial winds up and martial explodes; they can get on each other's nerves. (When someone has both influences internally, as Steve Jobs did, it can lead to abrasive restlessness.) Jovial and venusian are both passive and positive, and mildly repel. Lunar, the least developed type, can be repelled by jovial, the most developed.

16 ♡ YOUR "TYPE"

Many people have a "type," a physical and sometimes personality style that turns them on, a picture of what their ideal mate would look like. This can come from many places, including body-type attraction and many of the other factors covered in this book. For example, someone with a lunar body type might be attracted to people who are tall because the opposite body type, saturnian, tends to be tall (although there are short saturnians and tall people of other body types).

Someone might be attracted to blonds because her father was one. Hair color can also represent an emotional quality we like: blond feels cooler, and red, hotter. There might also be an indirect body-type correlation. Red hair color and skin tones are especially linked to martial bodies. An above-average number of solars have blond hair, whereas venusians are more often dark.

There are several reasons someone might be strongly attracted to women with large breasts: His mother or a movie star he fixated on when he was young might have had them. They may symbolize nurturing. And venusians tend to be large-breasted, so martials tend to be drawn to them.

16 YOUR "TYPE"

On a personality level, someone's type may be quiet people with a wry sense of humor because her father was like that, or extroverts because his mother was one (or because he's an introvert and it balances him). Some people are turned on by high intelligence because they like to be intellectually engaged.

If a relationship ended in a way that left us feeling incomplete, we might continue to look for someone resembling the person we lost so that we can find a sense of completion. Traumatic incompletions can be carried forward from past lives. For example, if the love of someone's life died young and she missed him for the rest of that lifetime, she might continue to look for him reincarnated or someone like him.

I have a Caucasian friend who is most strongly attracted to black men: she feels safe with them and doesn't with white men. In her experience, white men have been abusive, and black men, kind. Her first love was black, and no doubt there's also a past-life story or two here. Many metaphysical teachings say that we create our reality from our beliefs. Perhaps her beliefs about black and white men have drawn experiences that reinforce them.

In order to help us find a person with whom we have an important mate agreement, our soul may plant some clues in our subconscious. A friend said that she always knew she would marry a man with a deep voice, and sure enough, she's with an entity mate (a member of her spiritual family) who's a basso profundo. Pheromones (chemicals our body secretes) and other body scents can be more subtle clues that our subconscious picks up on to direct us to key people. We may fall for people who look or feel similar until we find the right one.

There's a Rodgers and Hart song, "You Always Love the Same Girl." Have you ever noticed how people's significant others tend to resemble one another in certain ways? I know someone whose first and second wives were born two days apart and both are blondes (as was his mother). Observing repetitive patterns in our life can be illuminating.

A person's type can simply be someone like him. Couples who do well together often look alike, perhaps like male and female versions of the same person. They seem to belong together, a matched set like salt and pepper shakers. The similarities most often show up in their faces. Couples can also increasingly resemble each other the longer they're together as they blend their energies. Opposites attract, but similarities bring comfort. Every relationship is a combination of opposites and similarities, although the proportion of each varies. Those who like more opposite traits especially enjoy excitement. Even couples who look alike in many ways can also have some

16 YOUR "TYPE"

striking opposites, such as one being tall and the other, short.

We sometimes hear of people falling in love with someone who isn't their type or those who don't have a type, which illustrates that there are many other factors that can bring people together. To some degree, we can transcend a lack of body-type attraction or the fact that someone isn't our type if there's enough that's compelling on other levels.

17 ♡ SEXUAL ORIENTATION

The most basic question of attraction is whether we're attracted to male or female bodies, or both.

LGBTQ

Some people object to exploring why LGBTQ people are not heterosexual and/or not identified with their birth sex, since few ask why straight cisgendered people are straight and cisgendered, but I am gay and I don't object to this line of questioning. We discussed defaults in the Introduction, including the fact that there is nothing sacred about them—they're simply where

17 SEXUAL ORIENTATION

we go when we don't have a reason not to. As mentioned, biology's default is heterosexuality—biology is a big fan of reproduction since it helps species survive. When the world's human population was low, the heterosexual default was probably stronger than it is today.

In *Messages from Michael*, Michael said, "All of you will have homosexual lives." Being LGBTQ is an interesting physical plane experience, offering different kinds of lessons from being strictly heterosexual/cisgendered, including the challenges of going against cultural norms. It's also a way to experience different kinds of energy flows.

We discussed multi-causality in the Introduction. There's usually more than one factor contributing to why someone is LGBTQ, but as mentioned, soul factors usually predominate. Souls planning a gay lifetime may also choose imprinting, body types, and other genetics that support that. (Males with feminine body types and females with masculine ones are slightly more inclined to be gay.)

As Freud suggested, early-childhood imprinting can be a factor in orientation, but it's unlikely to be the only one—if it doesn't reinforce soul-level factors, it's probably not going to sway one's orientation much. It's true, for example, that a boy with a missing or withdrawn father may so long for him that he fixates sexually on males. If, however, soul factors strongly lean toward being straight, that issue is likely to manifest in a different way.

WHY WE'RE ATTRACTED

We are imprinted by our parents' issues and expectations even in the womb, like applications installed on a computer's hard drive at the factory. The soul might erase them later but it usually just works around them, provided that enough space on the drive is available for its purposes, since that's less trouble.

An example is a male carried by a mother who wanted a girl. The imprint, if strong, may contribute to him being gay and/or feminine, especially if that suits the soul's purposes—imprinting for which a soul has an affinity is what is most likely to stick. If it doesn't have that affinity, the soul may try to erase or at least reduce it. Feminine traits that show up in childhood may recede as the soul asserts itself, and he might grow up identified as male and straight. Alternately, being bisexual and/or mildly feminine might still allow him to complete his soul-level tasks. Strong imprinting, however, can be a formidable obstacle and sometimes souls don't have the skill to overcome it.

The soul usually has a good idea before birth of what its imprinting will be like during the first few years of life. Even if some of it is undesirable, if the overall situation mostly works, the soul may be willing to accept and deal with the elements that don't—there are always compromises. Ultimately, it's all good, because every situation offers

17 SEXUAL ORIENTATION

opportunities to grow, but some are more uncomfortable than others.

Some souls prefer incarnating as males but occasionally need to develop balance by being female. Their previous attractions may not turn on a dime and they may continue to be attracted mostly to females (and/or to identify to some extent as male). After a lifetime or two in a female body, they might start to develop more sexual interest in males. Vice versa for souls who prefer incarnating as females.

A soul may have had traumatic experiences that damaged its masculine or feminine side. Let's say that in a past life, a man committed brutal acts of which he felt deeply conflicted and ashamed, and he associated them with being a man. He was then born in this lifetime as a male carrying the belief that men are violent and that it's bad to be a man, causing him to want to emulate the feminine, at the same time longing to find true manhood. This dilemma encourages him to deal with and hopefully resolve the issue.

Illustrating multi-causality, let's say that the soul also chose a dominant mother, making it easier to identify with her. That may further influence him toward being gay and/or feminine. Someone without wounded masculinity might not be as susceptible to identifying with her. Psychologists observe the dominant mother and assume that she is the cause of her son's homosexuality.

Without knowledge of the soul, they may not have a basis for understanding why that child resonated with her and accepted her imprinting in that way, whereas his brother didn't. There is always at least some symbiosis in such things.

There is a higher incidence of homosexuality in identical twins because they are used to bonding strongly with each other. Sometimes, however, one twin is gay and the other is straight, which shows that neither imprinting nor biology necessarily govern. Incidentally, identical twins don't always have identical body types, either, showing how our soul can meet different needs from the same raw material.

A study found that the hypothalamus (in the brain) is smaller in women and gay men than it is in heterosexual men. Some people concluded that sexual orientation is biological. Although biology can be a factor, it's more likely that the size of the hypothalamus as well as hormone levels are a result of how much they're used, due to soul and personality factors, rather than the cause.

The emergence of transgender issues has brought with it an awareness that gender identity isn't the same as sexual orientation. Someone born male, for example, may identify as female and be attracted to females. Like everyone else, transgendered people can be attracted to males, females, or both.

17 SEXUAL ORIENTATION

Transgendered people often had set up their upcoming lifetime to be one sex and at the last minute, took a body that was the other. In most cases, souls adjust to this change fairly easily, but sometimes they don't, especially if most of their recent lifetimes had been in the opposite sex body.

Probably more people are LGBTQ than is commonly thought; the stigma often leads to people not being honest about it, even with themselves, and certainly not with polling organizations. LGBTQ feminine men and masculine women cannot easily hide it. However, it is likely that the majority of LGBTQ people do not fit the stereotypes and are not discerned by the average person.

The world of male professional sports, for example, has been seen as being ultra-straight; only a few players have very recently come out. However, a male acquaintance dated an NFL football player and said that about 30% of his team was gay. Maybe there was some wishful thinking involved but chances are that in any group of people, a fairly high number of them are not straight. Many movie stars have been quietly known to be gay or bisexual, and gradually the public is realizing it. When a critical mass of celebrities comes out, it will no longer seem like a big deal.

BISEXUALITY

In *Messages from Michael*, Michael said that there are older souls "who have lost their strong sense of gender identity and have freed themselves up to love whoever comes along in whatever way seems most appropriate at the present moment." After all their lifetimes as both male and female, they are less identified with the body they happen to wear at the moment, and they respond to the soul in other people rather than to the body. That might be the ideal. We can't make ourselves feel that way if we don't, but I know some predominantly straight and gay people who have deliberately opened themselves to bisexuality in an attempt to break down their barriers. They may not have stuck with it long-term but feel that it enriched them, helping them become more balanced.

17 SEXUAL ORIENTATION

Sarah Chambers, the first Michael channel, channeled something to the effect that all female bodies have the hardwiring to be bisexual, perhaps because the feminine is responsive and can respond to either male or female, and that 25% of males do (in addition to those who are gay). Bisexuality does seem to be more common among women.

This implies the fascinating idea that sexual orientation has both a "hardware" and "software" component. The hardware (biological and energetic) factors include genetics, body type, and how the endocrine and nervous systems are configured. The software factors include, most importantly, the soul's history and intentions, as well as cultural and family imprinting. They determine how the person in the body actually wants to use its capabilities. This suggests that even if a soul isn't strongly identified with his body, if the body is male and is hardwired solely for heterosexuality (or homosexuality), the man won't be bisexual.

A surprising number of people who identify as being gay or straight have enjoyed bisexual experiences that they think "don't count" or feel they need to keep secret so as not to jeopardize their standing in their community. For example, some politically active feminist lesbians fear they would be ostracized if it were discovered that they sometimes slept with men. Some men on the "down-low" think of themselves as straight because they only "top." Many people are truly only straight or gay, but some are bisexual despite their identification.

The definition of bisexuality is hard to pin down. Most people could derive some pleasure from the touch of either sex such as when receiving a massage. There's a gray area between the therapeutic and the sensual. If someone is aroused when receiving a massage from someone of the same sex, does that alone make her bisexual or gay? Probably not. If someone enjoys it when a person of the same sex performs oral sex on him, does that make him bisexual or gay? Maybe not—it depends on whether the gender of the person is material to his arousal. Perhaps a realistic definition of bisexuality is that a person can be aroused by the bodies of either sex, as opposed to simply deriving pleasure from being stimulated.

There is a spectrum of bisexuality, from being a little bi but otherwise straight or gay to 50-50. A person's place on that spectrum is not necessarily fixed—it can fluctuate depending upon the circumstances and what's happening internally. Many can easily be monogamous with either a male or female, but some need both at the same time.

Bisexuality is often unconscious until something activates it and brings it to the surface. It can be limited to one or a few sexual activities or it can be

17 SEXUAL ORIENTATION

as fully engaged as the sexuality of a straight or gay person. Some women, for example, like to be with other women only above the waist. Some men won't kiss another man—it has to be purely sexual, without emotional attachment or romanticism, which they reserve for women. This may help them preserve the idea that they're not gay, just fooling around, or it may indicate that they have physical but not emotional attraction to men.

Sometimes, people fixate emotionally on the same sex but physically, on the opposite sex, or vice versa. For instance, a woman may emotionally want to be mated with another woman but her body responds more to men. Conversely, she may be more physically excited by women but feel that something is missing and find men more fulfilling emotionally and/or intellectually. Perhaps their emotional needs can be fulfilled through friendships. If not, and if this can't be worked out in therapy or otherwise, one solution might be to mate with a male/female couple with a bisexual member (see the next section on "Polyfidelity").

Some gay and straight people don't like to kiss or be romantic, either, often due to fear of intimacy. Many sex workers won't kiss their clients because they reserve that for someone with whom they're emotionally involved. They associate kissing with relationship, not just sex.

In general, artisans, sages, and priests are more romantic than the other roles. Warriors and kings tend to be matter-of-fact about sex and most other things, and can distrust what they perceive as excessive floridity. Scholars are often game for anything, but their neutrality doesn't naturally lean them toward romanticism. Servers appreciate romanticism—a small gesture often means a lot to them—but they're big on "first things first": basic needs take precedence for them.

18 ♡ MONOGAMY AND POLYFIDELITY

Polyfidelity is a term that refers to committed long-term relationships with more than one person as an alternative to monogamy, promiscuity, and swinging. These units of three or more can be straight, bisexual, or gay. (For more information on it, go to http://www.lovemore.com.) I suspect that we'll be seeing a lot more polyfidelitous relationships in coming decades.

Many people aren't suited to monogamy. There is much lip service given to it but in practice, often people "cheat." The use of that word shows how emotionally charged our imprinting is, but the idea that monogamy is the only moral lifestyle is a social construct; many societies feel differently. In some tribes, for instance, a woman may feel put upon if her husband has only one wife—she has to do all the housework! Although it's been historically more common for a man to be with more than one woman rather than the other way around, today there are increasing instances of a woman with more than one man, or two or more couples mated to each other. Due to China's one-child policy, there are now thirty million more adult men than women, and polyfidelity is being proposed as a solution. If someone is agonizing about choosing from more than one mate possibility, sometimes the answer might be "and" rather than "or." Or as I've joked, "Get a bigger bed!" However, it takes a great deal of maturity to make such relationships work.

Sometimes there are soul-level agreements that compel people to share something intimate outside their primary relationship. There's brainwashing in our society that brings, unquestioningly, the assumption that a partner being "unfaithful" is the greatest of betrayals. Therefore, someone who has committed to monogamy but who is not suited to it is in a tough quandary. Deceit is poisonous to a relationship, yet telling the truth can also destroy it, as can not being true to oneself. It might be cleaner to renegotiate agreements or end the relationship before seeking outside it.

Still, affairs are seldom premeditated, and expecting people, especially when they feel their needs aren't being met, to consistently have the self-discipline to decline a strong attraction may not be realistic. Making too much out of it only aggravates the problem. The best way to avoid it is to let a potential partner know at the beginning our stand on monogamy, whether we require it, aren't suited to it, or are open on the subject. If his stand is opposite, it might be better not to pursue the relationship further. A person may not realize his true needs when he's young, and needs can change over time. However, when people are honest and realistic about their needs before embarking upon a relationship, a lot of heartache can be avoided.

CONCLUSION

When we find someone attractive who doesn't reciprocate, it's easy to doubt our attractiveness, but as we've been exploring, what turns on another person is complex and isn't something we can control. When people are fortunate enough to find each other highly attractive and are able to make a relationship work, there's more than a little bit of luck involved.

Attraction brings people together but doesn't necessarily keep them together. Common interests allow for things to discuss and do together, and common values are even more important for relationship longevity. Unresolved issues between people can kill attraction as anger and resentment build up. Creating a strong relationship takes commitment, a mature ability to resolve conflicts and communicate clearly, and an alignment of purpose. A sense of humor helps, too.

Attraction can fade over time for many possible reasons. It may be that a couple completed their work together or that they fell into a rut and went on automatic pilot. Once the biological imperatives have been satisfied by successfully bringing mates together, there is less assistance from the chemical highs with which the body rewards us. If we have been doing the work of building a relationship, a deeper and more subtle love can develop. One indication of loving

CONCLUSION

someone in this way is enjoying being with him even when we're not getting something. In my experience, it takes at least six months to develop an energetic bond with someone, and it's been said that it takes seven years to become truly married. In any case, it takes time to grow mature love for a person, but it is well worth the effort.

Whether or not we currently are in a romantic relationship, the important thing is that we love in the highest way we know how, through all the avenues available to us. Expressing mature love and its attendant qualities such as truth, vitality, and creativity, is the highest achievement.

May you find joy in your relating!

ABOUT THE AUTHOR

SHEPHERD HOODWIN has been channeling since 1986. He also does intuitive readings, mediumship, past-life regression, healing, counseling, and channeling coaching (teaching others to channel). He has conducted workshops on the Michael teachings throughout the United States and Europe.

ABOUT THE AUTHOR

Shepherd is a graduate of the University of Oregon. He lives in Laguna Niguel, California.

https://shepherdhoodwin.com

TWITTER:
@shepherdh
@EnlightenNitwit

FACEBOOK:
https://www.facebook.com/shepherd.hoodwin
https://www.facebook.com/shepherd.hoodwin.author/
https://www.facebook.com/JourneyOfYourSoul/
https://www.facebook.com/EnlightenmentforNitwits/

shepherdhoodwin@gmail.com

Summerjoy Press
99 Pearl
Laguna Niguel CA 92677-4818

OTHER BOOKS BY SHEPHERD HOODWIN

Available at https://shepherdhoodwin.com/book/

All Is Choice

Few realize how profound, multi-faceted, and far-reaching the concept of choice is in our spiritual growth. This short book explores topics such as what is and is not our right to choose, our power as creators and the limits of our reality creation, how consciousness expands, and much more.

Being in the World

This insightful book explores practical spirituality. Topics include aging, karma, time, and religion.

Compassion for Evil
A Metaphysical View

Compassion for Evil explores the nature of evil from the soul's point of view, and how we can skillfully deal with it as lightworkers.

Embracing What Is
Spiritual Keys to Happiness

This book is an abridged version of *Happiness and the Michael Teachings*, without technical Michael teachings terminology. A free version is available at Smashwords.com.

OTHER BOOKS BY SHEPHERD HOODWIN

Energy Literacy
How to Perceive and Take Charge of Your Spiritual Well-Being

Energy Literacy is an introduction to how to perceive our energy field and release negativity. Topics include chakras, contracts, vows, cording, entities, implants, psychic attack, earthbound souls, soul retrieval, and more.

Enlightenment for Nitwits
The Complete Guide

This hilarious metaphysical/self-help humor collection will appeal to Oprah and Dave Barry fans as well as those with more esoteric interests. In a style reminiscent of comedian Steven Wright, it's full of wry one-liners along with longer, hilariously mind-bending pieces on a wide range of subjects, tied together by the idea of clueless humans trying to find enlightenment.

"I love *Enlightenment for Nitwits*! It is the funniest book I have read in several decades. If laughter leads to enlightenment, it will certainly do it. Nothing—thank God—is sacred in this delightful spoof on life in general."

—C. Norman Shealy, M.D., author of *Life Beyond 100*

Growing Through Joy

This thought-provoking book explores the nature of personal growth.

Happiness and the Michael Teachings
Learning to Embrace What Is

Happiness is the ultimate goal of every spiritual teaching. Here we explore several principles of what the Michael teachings refer to as growing through joy.

Healing the Gut
A Crib Sheet for Eliminating SIBO

This short ebook offers tips for those with digestive problems and related diseases, focusing on the Specific Carbohydrate Diet.

Journey of Your Soul
A Channel Explores the Michael Teachings

This is the most in-depth discussion of the Michael teachings to date. It may also be the first analytical study of channeling written by a channel. It has forewords by John Friedlander, co-author of *Psychic Psychology*, and Jon Klimo, author of *Channeling: Investigations on Receiving Information from Paranormal Sources*. Klimo writes, "*Journey of Your Soul* may well be the best (Michael) book of them all due to its clarity, thoroughness, and detail, and thanks to the fact that the author, an exceptionally clear-headed

Michael channel himself, brings real integrity and authenticity to our understanding of Michael in particular and to the channeling process in general."

Loving from Your Soul
Creating Powerful Relationships

This inspiring, transformative book explores the nature of love itself as well as practical matters of relationships. One reader wrote, "There are phrases that are so inspiring that I wrote them down to refer to when I need them. I am looking forward to reading this book again and again."

Meditations for Self-Discovery
Guided Journeys for Communicating with Your Inner Self

This is a beautiful collection of forty-five vivid, often pastoral, guided imagery meditations channeled from Shepherd's essence. There are many meditation recordings available, but this is one of the first collections of meditations in book form that can be read to oneself or others. Teachers and group leaders would find it particularly useful.

Opening to Healing

This uplifting book explores the spiritual aspect of healing.

Unconditional Love in Politics
Or Have You Hugged a Republican/Democrat Today?

Is unconditional love in politics an oxymoron? Thus far, it's been a rare commodity if it's ever been there. This book explores what you can do about it, as well as why both right and left have useful parts to play in our evolution, the factors that influence a person's tilt to the right or left, and what unconditional love might look like in this sphere.

REVIEWS

I couldn't put it down. Bravo!

EVERYONE SHOULD READ *WHY WE'RE ATTRACTED*!!! Clear understanding of one of the everlasting enigmas of life! Far better than Freud or any other psychologist.
—C. Norman Shealy, M.D., Ph.D., author of *Living*

This book contains so much valuable information and is just what I needed to read.

Wonderful!

Printed in Great Britain
by Amazon